Vero Beach Memories

A Photo Retrospective of Vero Beach and Indian River County

Presented by **GHO HOMES** WWW.GHOHOMES.COM *and brought to you by*  **Press Journal** INDIAN RIVER | TCPALM.COM

ACKNOWLEDGMENTS

Indian River Press Journal/TCPalm and is pleased to present "Vero Beach Memories: A Photo Retrospective of Vero Beach and Indian River County." It must be noted, however, that this unique pictorial history book would not have been possible without the generous contributions made by many people from virtually every corner of the community.

We are indebted, first of all, to those early area residents who captured their time—our history—in photographs, and provided a glimpse into their lives.

Secondly, all area residents are indebted to the many individuals who are committed to preserving our history in various libraries, historical societies, archives and personal collections throughout our community.

The following organizations and people have contributed greatly to this project:

The Indian River County Historical Society Board of Directors and its Archival Committee:
Carolyn Bayless, Alma Lee Loy, Janice Sellers, Mary Frances Womack,
and Ruth Stanbridge, County Historian.

Archive Center at the Indian River County Main Library:
Dru Skinner, Brenda Corum, Chuck Balius, Susan Barker, Marvin Carter, Marcia Eyberse,
Marjorie Jackson, Richard Bolinger, Gale Parmetier, Sharon Pike and Ed Elliot.

From the team at the Press Journal for their efforts in coordination, promotion and sales:
Marketing Director Rick Baxter, Inez Frid, Holly Johansen, Carol Archebelle, and visuals editor Kelly Rogers.

FOREWORD

The history that surrounds a community isn't just about newsworthy events or famous people, nor is it just about development and industry. At its core, history is about the people. The people who when they first came to the area had a vision, and then endeavored to build it. The pioneer spirit, or as it's often reference it today, the entrepreneurial spirit is the true essence of the people of Indian River County and its communities.

Vero Beach Memories is a pictorial representation of Indian River County, but essentially it's a celebration of the people and the communities they built.

The book features photos that reveal the story of Vero Beach and Indian River County in hundreds of captivating images. We went through hundreds of images. Many came straight out of their frames, others from dusty shoe boxes, and others still from photo albums and attics. But the majority came from a partnership between the Press Journal with the Indian River Historical Society and the Indian River County Library. Overall there were more than 30 contributors from the community. The result, 250 photos that tell the story of Indian River County.

In addition to the assistance received from the Indian River Historical Society, the Indian River County Library and of the many readers who opened their personal collections and memories to share with others, I would like to personally thank GHO Homes for sponsoring this beautiful book. Established in 1983, award winning GHO Homes is committed to the area just as it is committed to the highest quality of craftsmanship and design of family-focused homes and communities.

We hope you enjoy and reflect on these photos, as much as we did in compiling this book.

Bob Brunjes
President and Publisher
Indian River Press Journal and TCPalm

WRITING TREASURE COAST HISTORY...
ONE COMMUNITY AT A TIME!

GHO Homes is honored to be part of Vero Beach's history as well as part of it's future. The GHO Homes team has been building in Vero Beach for over 20 years and is currently building in over 15 communities in Indian River County. GHO Homes not only develops new communities and completes existing ones, but has a robust Build-On-Your-Lot program.

GHO Homes takes pride in their construction quality, values, attention to detail, Tailor Made options program and commitment to the Treasure Coast.

In 2015 – to further define that commitment – GHO Homes opened their state-of-the-art 3,500 square foot Design Studio in Vero Beach.

Visit GHOHomes.com for more information on homes priced from the low $200s to $900s.

GHO HOMES

772.257.1100   ghohomes.com

INDIAN RIVER
Press Journal

COVERING LOCAL NEWS AND INFORMATION SINCE 1919

Each day, a new day dawns with the opportunity for the Indian River Press Journal to tell the story of the people and the places of wonderful Indian River County. Over a lifetime, or two, or three, those stories comprise a history of this place that we treasure as our community and call home.

Since the time that Vero was simply known as Vero, and before it was even Indian River County, the Press Journal has taken its promise to cover local news very seriously. For nearly 100 years the Press Journal has become an institution in the Indian River County community by growing along with it.

In 1919 we started in the center of where it all started, downtown on Seminole Avenue. Today, 96 years later, we moved back to Downtown, this time to the Seminole Building.

Press Journal
Friday, May 6, 1927

Vero Press
September 13, 1918

TABLE OF CONTENTS

CHAPTER ONE
VIEWS AND STREET SCENES

Look up and down the streets around you, what do you see? Traffic, storefronts, unique signage, old hotels, historic buildings? Familiar faces? How about all of the above.

In places like Vero Beach, Sebastian and Fellsmere. Or Indian River Shores, Roseland, Wabasso and Winter Beach you see the lifeblood of a community hustling through its now asphalt arteries. In every street scene, familiar sights and scenes are offered up, many of which have been a part of each of these communities history since the early pioneers settled here and shaped the neighborhoods we see today.

As you are looking through these pages, take note of those familiar scenes. While the mode of transportation has changed over the years, many of the streets, intersections and buildings are still recognizable today and that can be attributed to the importance of history and preservation to the people of Indian River County.

OPPOSITE: A view of downtown Vero Beach looking north on 14th Avenue, circa 1960. Osceola Pharmacy and Rexall Drug Store, Indian River Citrus Bank, and Standard Oil Gasoline Station are visible near the intersection of 20th Street. COURTESY INDIAN RIVER COUNTY HISTORICAL SOCIETY COLLECTION, ARCHIVE CENTER, INDIAN RIVER COUNTY MAIN LIBRARY

LEFT: A view of Seminole Avenue (14th Avenue), in Vero, early 1920s. Gilman's Restaurant, Vero Theatre, Drugstore, Western Union and Farmer's Bank can be seen. COURTESY SMITH COLLECTION, ARCHIVE CENTER, INDIAN RIVER COUNTY MAIN LIBRARY

OPPOSITE TOP LEFT: An westward view of Osceola Blvd. (20th Street) in the early 1920s. Lebos Shoe and Dry Goods, Illinois Hotel, and the Maher's building are visible on the left. At the far left side is Dr. Grossman's house which later became the Cox and Floyd Funeral Home. COURTESY INDIAN RIVER COUNTY HISTORICAL SOCIETY COLLECTION, ARCHIVE CENTER, INDIAN RIVER COUNTY MAIN LIBRARY

OPPOSITE TOP RIGHT: A westward view of downtown Vero (Seminole Avenue (14th Avenue) and Route 60) in the later 1920s. The Osceola Apartment building is on the right side, built circa 1927. A drug store, Jun's Grocery, and Maher's Department Store are also among the businesses pictured. COURTESY INDIAN RIVER COUNTY HISTORICAL SOCIETY COLLECTION, ARCHIVE CENTER, INDIAN RIVER COUNTY MAIN LIBRARY

OPPOSITE BOTTOM: A view of Main Street (Old Dixie) in Quay (Winter Beach), circa 1915. The building at left was owned by John M. McCullers, Sr. and had living quarters on the second floor and a store on the first floor. COURTESY JANET ANDERSON

ABOVE: View looking over Liberty Park from the original Seminole building on Seminole Ave (14th Ave) and 21st Street, circa 1925. COURTESY INDIAN RIVER COUNTY HISTORICAL SOCIETY COLLECTION, ARCHIVE CENTER, INDIAN RIVER COUNTY MAIN LIBRARY

ABOVE LEFT: A southward view down Seminole Avenue (14th Avenue) in the 1920s. The Vero Theatre, Vero Restaurant, United Cigars, Farmers Bank, and a drugstore are visible. COURTESY INDIAN RIVER COUNTY HISTORICAL SOCIETY COLLECTION, ARCHIVE CENTER, INDIAN RIVER COUNTY MAIN LIBRARY

LEFT: Seminole Avenue (14th Avenue) and Osceola Blvd. (20th Street), Vero, circa 1920s. "No U Turns" stand in middle of intersection. Farmer's bank, Vero Theater, Western Union and Liberty Park are shown. COURTESY INDIAN RIVER COUNTY HISTORICAL SOCIETY COLLECTION, ARCHIVE CENTER, INDIAN RIVER COUNTY MAIN LIBRARY

OPPOSITE: The Pocahontas Building, located on the corner of Seminole Avenue (14th Avenue) and 21st Street, in 1925. Lettering on the roof reads "Vero Press". To the west is construction of the Campbell Arcade, a two-story building which housed the Vero Beach Arcade and King's Diner Dance Hall. It burned down in 2005. COURTESY INDIAN RIVER COUNTY HISTORICAL SOCIETY COLLECTION, ARCHIVE CENTER, INDIAN RIVER COUNTY MAIN LIBRARY

ABOVE: The Florida Theatre, located in the center of the block on 14th Avenue between 20th and 21st streets, circa 1940s. Seminole building is on the far end.
COURTESY INDIAN RIVER COUNTY HISTORICAL SOCIETY COLLECTION, ARCHIVE CENTER, INDIAN RIVER COUNTY MAIN LIBRARY

ABOVE RIGHT: The Farmer's Bank building, located on the corner of Seminole Avenue (14th Avenue) and Osceola Boulevard (20th Street), circa 1930s. The first bank was originally built in 1914 for $7,000. In 1925, it was completely redone by architect Frederick H. Trimble and contractor J.H. Baker. It closed during the depression and reopened in 1935 as Indian River Citrus Bank. Western Union is visible on the left.
COURTESY INDIAN RIVER COUNTY HISTORICAL SOCIETY COLLECTION, ARCHIVE CENTER, INDIAN RIVER COUNTY MAIN LIBRARY

RIGHT: 14th Street, Vero Beach, circa 1940s. Businesses include Piggly Wiggly, DuBose Jewelry Company, the Florida Theatre and Wodtke's Department Store. COURTESY INDIAN RIVER PRESS JOURNAL

OPPOSITE: Osceola Blvd (20th Street), looking eastward toward the Maher Building, Vero Beach, circa 1938. COURTESY JACKIE VITEK

ABOVE: An eastward view of Osceola Apartments on 20th Street at the corner of 15th Avenue, circa 1940s. Herman J. Zeuch, the original owner, named the building.
COURTESY INDIAN RIVER COUNTY HISTORICAL SOCIETY COLLECTION, ARCHIVE CENTER, INDIAN RIVER COUNTY MAIN LIBRARY

RIGHT: Downtown Vero Beach, circa 1940s. COURTESY INDIAN RIVER PRESS JOURNAL

ABOVE: An eastward view of 20th Street (SR 60) in Vero Beach, in the 1940s.
COURTESY SMITH COLLECTION, ARCHIVE CENTER, INDIAN RIVER COUNTY MAIN LIBRARY

LEFT: A view of the corner of 14th Avenue and 20th Street in Vero Beach in the 1940s. COURTESY SMITH COLLECTION, ARCHIVE CENTER, INDIAN RIVER COUNTY MAIN LIBRARY

ABOVE: Street view of the intersection of 14th Avenue and 20th Street in Vero Beach, late 1940s. Rexall Drugs on left. At right is Indian River Citrus Bank, W. W. Mag Co., the Florida Theatre, and the Seminole Building
COURTESY SMITH COLLECTION, ARCHIVE CENTER, INDIAN RIVER COUNTY MAIN LIBRARY

ABOVE RIGHT: Luke Knight Fruit Stand at 45th Street and US Hwy. 1, Gifford, 1949. COURTESY JAY C. MILLER

RIGHT: A southward view of 20th Street in the early 1950s. A gift shop, Amoco Gasoline Station, the Maher's building, city water tower, and Hotel Luther are visible.
COURTESY INDIAN RIVER PRESS JOURNAL

OPPOSITE: A bird's-eye view of Sexton Plaza (lower foreground) and Ocean Drive, circa 1955. The building at the southeast end of the plaza is Ocean Grill. A large swimming pool is visible at the plaza's north end.
COURTESY INDIAN RIVER COUNTY HISTORICAL SOCIETY COLLECTION, ARCHIVE CENTER, INDIAN RIVER COUNTY MAIN LIBRARY

ABOVE: Street view of the intersection of 14th Avenue and 20th Street in Vero Beach, late 1950s.
COURTESY SMITH COLLECTION, ARCHIVE CENTER, INDIAN RIVER COUNTY MAIN LIBRARY

LEFT: A view looking south down 14th Avenue toward SR 60 in downtown Vero Beach in the mid-1950s. Wodtke's Department Store is at right.
COURTESY SUSAN WODTKE SMITH

OPPOSITE: Municipal Park and Beach in Vero Beach in the early 1950s. COURTESY SMITH COLLECTION, ARCHIVE CENTER, INDIAN RIVER COUNTY MAIN LIBRARY

CHAPTER TWO

TRANSPORTATION

Think planes trains and automobiles, but it wasn't always that way. Imagine paddle wheels, sailboats and schooners travelling along the Indian River, the area's first highway albeit a natural one.

In simpler times mule drawn carts moved produce to market and early model Fords moved people through town. But it was Henry Flagler and his Florida East Coast Railroad that inextricably changed the landscape forever. Without the railroad to transport crops of grapefruit and potatoes to out-of-area markets, or to bring the speculators and tourists in, Vero and surrounding areas would have been very different.

Not long after the railroad, automobiles found their way onto almost every driveway, Eastern Air Lines introduced passenger airline service and aircraft manufacturing came to the area, attesting to the notion that Vero Beach is always a city in motion.

OPPOSITE: Ribbon-cutting ceremony for service of new Streamliner, Florida East Coast Railway, Flagler System. Standing after children, from left: Elena K. Mead, Tom Trent, Marcel Boudet, Earl Thatcher, Lou Berger, Betty Jean Zigrang Hunt, unknown, Trucy Kromhout, Archie Adams.

COURTESY INDIAN RIVER COUNTY HISTORICAL SOCIETY COLLECTION, ARCHIVE CENTER, INDIAN RIVER COUNTY MAIN LIBRARY

ABOVE: The Florida East Coast Railway Depot on 69th Street and Main Street, Quay (Winter Beach), circa 1910. The town of Quay, was originally named Woodley until it was changed in 1902, in honor of Pennsylvania Senator Matthew S. Quay who introduced a Senate bill to widen and deepen the Intercoastal Waterway which the community thought would be of benefit. In 1922 the name of the community was changed, for promotional purposes to Winter Beach. In 1925, when Indian River County was established, Winter Beach almost became the county seat. But the town of Vero (now Vero Beach) was an incorporated city, and was selected as the county seat. COURTESY JANET ANDERSON

RIGHT: Three cars on Riverside Drive – Old U.S. Hwy. 1. Picture from portfolio of San Sebastain Development.
COURTESY INDIAN RIVER COUNTY HISTORICAL SOCIETY COLLECTION, ARCHIVE CENTER, INDIAN RIVER COUNTY MAIN LIBRARY

ABOVE: Bridge over the Main Relief canal, circa 1915. COURTESY INDIAN RIVER PRESS JOURNAL

ABOVE LEFT: On September 6, 1920, the first bridge across the Indian River from Sebastian to Jupiter opened on Labor Day. Over 300 cars attended the celebration to cross the bridge that required a toll. The Vero Beach Development Company of Cleveland, Ohio helped to finance the bridge for a very good reason. They were planning to build their winter homes in what is present day Riomar. COURTESY INDIAN RIVER COUNTY HISTORICAL SOCIETY COLLECTION, ARCHIVE CENTER, INDIAN RIVER COUNTY MAIN LIBRARY

LEFT: Fellsmere Railroad Depot, circa 1913. In the early days of the development of Fellsmere, the Fellsmere Railroad was the only way of conveniently getting to and from Fellsmere from Sebastian. The railroad was completed in September 1910 and the depot was built in 1913 by E.M. Botts of West Palm Beach. The 12-foot by 32-foot structure was located at the north end of Broadway in Fellsmere. COURTESY CLARENCE F. "KORKY" KORKER

ABOVE: Two men stand beside a Ford Model T, circa 1925. The buildings in the background are located on corner of Seminole Avenue (14th Avenue).
COURTESY INDIAN RIVER COUNTY HISTORICAL SOCIETY COLLECTION, ARCHIVE CENTER, INDIAN RIVER COUNTY MAIN LIBRARY

RIGHT: Two mechanics on a ladder attend to the right wing of a Ford Tri-Motor airplane, circa 1930. Two men in suit coats and fedoras and one woman wearing a long coat and cloche hat stand on the right.
COURTESY INDIAN RIVER COUNTY HISTORICAL SOCIETY COLLECTION, ARCHIVE CENTER, INDIAN RIVER COUNTY MAIN LIBRARY

BELOW: James D. Tew, President of B.F. Goodrich invited friends to enjoy flights in the Goodrich flagship "Miss Silverton" piloted by famous ace Lee Schoenhair (upper right), who flew at an air meet marking the opening of Vero Beach Municipal Airport in 1930. COURTESY INDIAN RIVER PRESS JOURNAL

ABOVE: The Optimist Club painting "Vero Beach" identification for air travel, 11th Avenue, 1928.
COURTESY INDIAN RIVER PRESS JOURNAL

LEFT: A high-wing, single-engine airplane with pontoons arrives at dock, circa 1940. Four men stand on the dock, ready to help secure the plane. COURTESY INDIAN RIVER COUNTY HISTORICAL SOCIETY COLLECTION, ARCHIVE CENTER, INDIAN RIVER COUNTY MAIN LIBRARY

ABOVE RIGHT: Speculators arrive at the Indian River Landing aboard the ATLANTIC, circa 1920s.

COURTESY INDIAN RIVER COUNTY HISTORICAL SOCIETY COLLECTION, ARCHIVE CENTER, INDIAN RIVER COUNTY MAIN LIBRARY

BELOW RIGHT: Alvin Carlsward and Carl Carlsward on a homemade vehicle on the Carlsward homestead on Barber Avenue, Vero Beach, 1936.

COURTESY MARILYN CARLSWARD INGRAM

OPPOSITE: Men survey the wreckage of an Eastern Air Lines crash on April 16, 1941, in a marsh west of Vero Beach. The crash was caused by a violent storm that reached tornado intensity about 9:00 a.m.

COURTESY INDIAN RIVER COUNTY HISTORICAL SOCIETY COLLECTION, ARCHIVE CENTER, INDIAN RIVER COUNTY MAIN LIBRARY

ABOVE: Several of the Dolphinettes are welcoming visitors with Indian RIver citrus at a Vero Beach Airport even in 1960 COURTESY INDIAN RIVER PRESS JOURNAL

ABOVE RIGHT: Mrs. A. W. Young, seated in a wheelchair, cuts the ribbon during the dedication ceremony for the Merrill Barber Bridge on March 18, 1951. COURTESY INDIAN RIVER COUNTY HISTORICAL SOCIETY COLLECTION, ARCHIVE CENTER, INDIAN RIVER COUNTY MAIN LIBRARY

RIGHT: E.G. Thatcher, unknown, Dorothy Wimbrow, WIlliam C. Wodtke,Sr. and S.V. (Stanley) Buss welcomes an Eastern Air Lines flight into Vero Beach in the 1950s. COURTESY SUSAN WODTKE SMITH

OPPOSITE TOP: A northeast view of the Merrill Barber Bridge on dedication day, March 18, 1951. Many people, automobiles, and flags can be seen on the bridge. COURTESY INDIAN RIVER COUNTY HISTORICAL SOCIETY COLLECTION, ARCHIVE CENTER, INDIAN RIVER COUNTY MAIN LIBRARY

OPPOSITE BOTTOM LEFT: Intersection of Seminole Avenue and Osceola Boulevard – Vero Beach Square. COURTESY INDIAN RIVER COUNTY HISTORICAL SOCIETY COLLECTION, ARCHIVE CENTER, INDIAN RIVER COUNTY MAIN LIBRARY

OPPOSITE BOTTOM RIGHT: Vera and Howard Ingells purchase Eastern Air Lines tickets at the Vero Beach Municipal Airport ticket counter, circa 1948. An employee of the airline (left) and Bud Hollman (right) stand of the other side of the counter. COURTESY INDIAN RIVER COUNTY HISTORICAL SOCIETY COLLECTION, ARCHIVE CENTER, INDIAN RIVER COUNTY MAIN LIBRARY

ABOVE: Tom Stewart loads Blue Goose Citrus onto an airplane as the stewardess and pilots look on, circa 1960.

ABOVE LEFT: Jeff Goddard (right) operates equipment at Vero Beach Eastern Air Lines terminal, circa 1960.

LEFT: Governor Fuller Warren stands on the wing of a South Dade Farms airplane, circa 1950s.

OPPOSITE: Vero Beach Municipal Airport at the 20th Anniversary celebration in 1952. L to R: Bud Holman, unknown, Ethel Gunner, Olive Smith, Kitty Warr, unknown on stairs, unknown woman, Bessie Dean Harris, unknown.

CHAPTER THREE

SCHOOLS AND EDUCATION

In 1824 Indian River County was named Mosquito County. As the name implies, forging a homestead was grueling. For the faint hearted, building roads and carving out canals from the tangle of coastal vegetation, and then grow crops and livestock in such an extreme environment would have been too arduous, impossible even. But not for the tenacious early settlers of Vero, they persevered and soon thereafter thrived.

Always with an eye to the future, not long after the basics were met, settlers started to build schools. Education was important. Simple structures at first, made only of palm trunks and fronds the one room school house started to dot the local landscape as early as 1880. The first such school house, the Orchid School, was on the barrier island.

The first brick schoolhouse, Vero Elementary, was built on the mainland in 1919 about the same time the first bridge was also built. Until then children had to cross the Indian River by boat.

OPPOSITE: Vero Beach Elementary School classroom in the 1950s. Student William Stanbridge at extreme left.

COURTESY INDIAN RIVER COUNTY HISTORICAL SOCIETY COLLECTION, ARCHIVE CENTER, INDIAN RIVER COUNTY MAIN LIBRARY

ABOVE: First Vero Elementary School under construction, circa 1919.
COURTESY INDIAN RIVER COUNTY HISTORICAL SOCIETY COLLECTION, ARCHIVE CENTER, INDIAN RIVER COUNTY MAIN LIBRARY

LEFT: A group of Vero Beach High School students in 1924 including members of the junior volleyball team.
COURTESY INDIAN RIVER COUNTY HISTORICAL SOCIETY COLLECTION, ARCHIVE CENTER, INDIAN RIVER COUNTY MAIN LIBRARY

OPPOSITE TOP LEFT: First-grade class at Vero Elementary School in 1924.
COURTESY HAFFIELD COLLECTION, ARCHIVE CENTER, INDIAN RIVER COUNTY MAIN LIBRARY

OPPOSITE TOP RIGHT: High School students, Vero, 1924.
COURTESY INDIAN RIVER COUNTY HISTORICAL SOCIETY COLLECTION, ARCHIVE CENTER, INDIAN RIVER COUNTY MAIN LIBRARY

OPPOSITE BOTTOM: Vero High School and Elementary Complex, circa 1920.
COURTESY INDIAN RIVER COUNTY HISTORICAL SOCIETY COLLECTION, ARCHIVE CENTER, INDIAN RIVER COUNTY MAIN LIBRARY

ABOVE: Mary Rodenberg and her class marching in parade carrying a sign that reads "The Most Efficient Nation 1950," circa 1920s.
COURTESY INDIAN RIVER COUNTY HISTORICAL SOCIETY COLLECTION, ARCHIVE CENTER, INDIAN RIVER COUNTY MAIN LIBRARY

RIGHT: Vero Beach High School students at a football game between Vero Beach and Ft. Pierce, Thanksgiving Day, November 28, 1940. Sponsors and escorts, front row, from left: Vera Crawford, senior; Bill Thatcher, junior; Madella Bunn, Class of 1939; Clark Rice Jr., Class of 1940.
COURTESY INDIAN RIVER COUNTY HISTORICAL SOCIETY COLLECTION, ARCHIVE CENTER, INDIAN RIVER COUNTY MAIN LIBRARY

OPPOSITE TOP: Vero Beach Elementary School play "Santa Claus in Mother Goose Land," December 21, 1928. COURTESY MARILYN CARLSWARD INGRAM

OPPOSITE BOTTOM LEFT: Vero Beach High School graduating Class of 1926. From left: Ruth Young, John Perritt, Louisa Vann, John Sullivan, E. Harris, William Routh, Lillian Gollnick, Arthur Hill, Rebecca Rodenberg, Erwin Jun, Marie Kellerman, James Reams, Louise Bunce, Carl Damerow, Bernita Whilden. COURTESY SHARON PIKE

OPPOSITE BOTTOM RIGHT: Mary Lou Anderson beside an Indian River County school bus in Winter Beach, circa 1948. COURTESY JANET ANDERSON

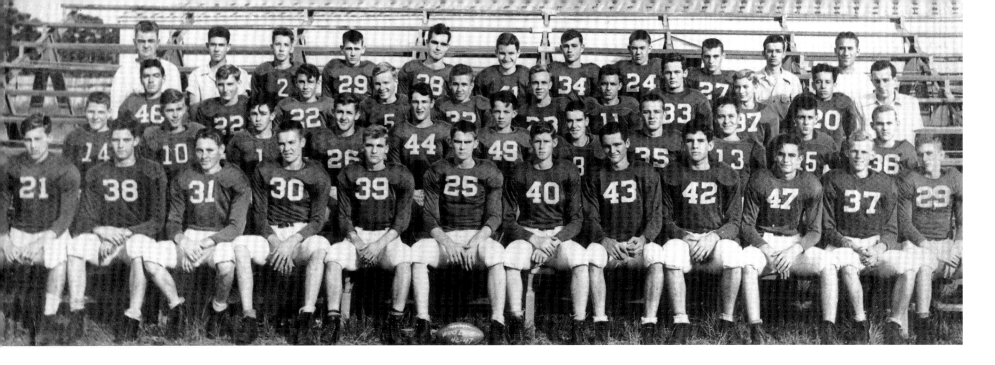

ABOVE: The first undefeated Vero Beach High School State Championship team, 1946. The team went 10-0 with a championship win of 39-0 over Lake Butler. The team scored 248 points compared to the opposition's 24. Team captain Herb "Bull" Henderson is third row, sixth from left. The team was coached by H. L. Wasson. First Row: 21-Robert Alison, 38-Curtis King, 31-David Prang, 30-Gene Carlsward, 39-Cecil Cason, 25-Richard Brown, 40-Sam McCall, 43-Robert Nelson, 42-Joel Parker, 47-Normand Mattmuller, 37-Bill Eubanks, 29-Everitt Randall; Second Row:14-Jack Smith, 10-Bill Davis, 1-Harry Swazy, 26-Bob Rice, 44-Art Snider, 49-Bob White, 8-Don McGinley, 35-Glenn Moon, 13-Charles Giffis, 5-Tom Moody, 36-Devie Bergren; Third Row:46-Bill Teat, 22-Pete MacWilliam, 22-Carl Elliot, 5-Jamie Buckingham, 32-Thom Kromhaut, 23-Bull Henderson, 11-Jack Graves, 33-V.L. Whittier, 37-John Bishop, 20-Frank Barret; Fourth Row:2-Bufford Ingraham, 29-Bob Lewis, 28-Bob Martin, 41-Pat Ercolin, 34-Bob Bass, 24-J.W. Calhoun, 27-Bill Rymer; Managers: Tom Holman, Norris Penland, Charles Smith; Coaches: H.L. Wasson, M.J. Cavana. COURTESY MIKE HENDERSON

RIGHT: Vero Beach Elementary School, third-grade class, with teacher Mrs. Regina Goddard, circa 1943.
COURTESY INDIAN RIVER COUNTY HISTORICAL SOCIETY COLLECTION, ARCHIVE CENTER, INDIAN RIVER COUNTY MAIN LIBRARY

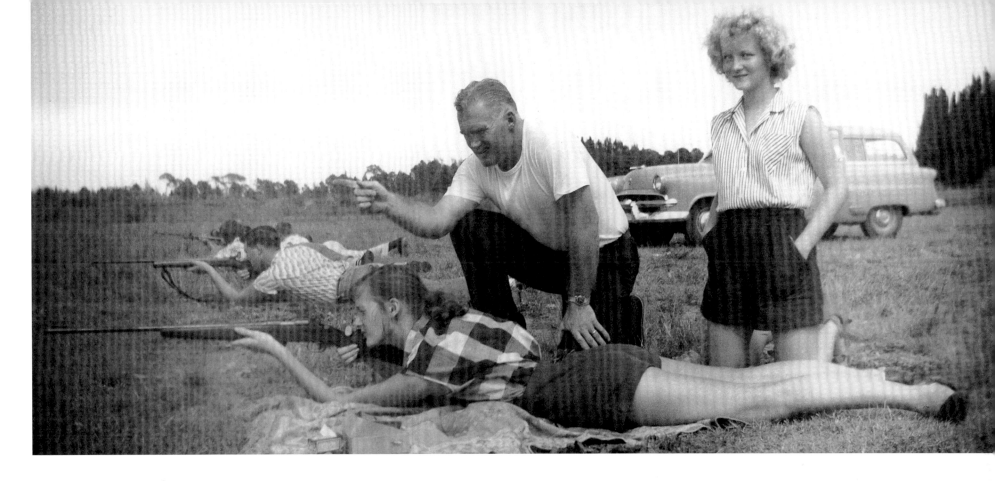

ABOVE: Tex Warrington, football coach at Vero Beach High School, coaching rifle practice.

COURTESY INDIAN RIVER COUNTY
HISTORICAL SOCIETY COLLECTION, ARCHIVE CENTER,
INDIAN RIVER COUNTY MAIN LIBRARY

LEFT: The 1946 Vero Beach High School State Championship football team's offensive lineup. Front row, from left: Curtis King, Joel Parker, B. L. Whittier, Glenn Moon, Sammy McCall, Robert Nelson, Bill Eubanks. Back row: Herb "Bull" Henderson, Bill Rhymer, Rob Rice, J. W. Calhoun.

COURTESY JACKIE VITEK

ABOVE: Mosquito identification training session at the Entomological Research Center, currently University of Florida: Florida Medical Entomology Laboratory. COURTESY UNIVERSITY OF FLORIDA

ABOVE RIGHT: Setting mosquito traps. Entomological Research Center, currently University of Florida: Florida Medical Entomology Laboratory. COURTESY UNIVERSITY OF FLORIDA

RIGHT: Dedication of the Entomological Research Center, currently University of Forida: Florida Medical Entomology Laboratory, 1956. COURTESY UNIVERSITY OF FLORIDA

ABOVE: Raising mosquitoes for research at the Entomological Research Center, currently University of Florida: Florida Medical Entomology Laboratory.
COURTESY UNIVERSITY OF FLORIDA

LEFT: Testing mosquito control fogging equipment at the Entomological Research Center, currently University of Florida: Florida Medical Entomology Laboratory.
COURTESY UNIVERSITY OF FLORIDA

ABOVE: Algebra II class taught by Mrs. Doris Lewis, Vero Beach High School, circa 1960. COURTESY INDIAN RIVER PRESS JOURNAL

OPPOSITE TOP: Vero Beach High School typing class in the late 1960s. COURTESY INDIAN RIVER PRESS JOURNAL

OPPOSITE BOTTOM LEFT: Winter Beach School students with teacher Mrs. Maggie Kersey in front of the school at the corner of 65th Street and US 1, circa 1960. Kneeling, from left: Virginia Anderson, Bunnie McNeal. Sitting: Shirley Bakes, Wendell Hinton, Joan Wynn, Leonard Garbett, Jody Sapp, Huey Walker, Melba Donaldson. Standing: Jessie Fendley, Barbara McCullers, unidentified, Mrs. Kersey, Wynn, unidentified, Kenneth "Tinker" McCullers. COURTESY JANET ANDERSON

OPPOSITE BOTTOM RIGHT: Baker Holland, Dwayne Morris, and other Future Farmers of America students. COURTESY INDIAN RIVER COUNTY HISTORICAL SOCIETY COLLECTION, ARCHIVE CENTER, INDIAN RIVER COUNTY MAIN LIBRARY

RIGHT: Basketball game featuring Vero Beach High School (in white), circa 1960s.

ABOVE: Vero Beach High School football team, December 1964.
COURTESY INDIAN RIVER PRESS JOURNAL

ABOVE LEFT: School children being shown a Press Journal typesetter machine, March 1961. COURTESY INDIAN RIVER PRESS JOURNAL

LEFT: Fellsmere Public School, circa 1968. The school was designed by former Methodist missionary architect, Frederick H. Trimble, in 1915. Arthur F. Sanders built the school in 1915-16 at a cost more than $40,000. On October 2, 1916, the school opened its doors to 136 students, one principal, one vice principal and five teachers for grades 1-12. The building was restored in 2010 and is now the Fellsmere City Hall and Boys and Girls Club.
COURTESY CLARENCE F. "KORKY" KORKER

CHAPTER FOUR

COMMERCE AND INDUSTRY

Citrus was the primary industry for many years and one that brought worldwide recognition to the area for its high quality. In fact, the colorful history of citrus in the area goes back to the 1800s and is just as important to the local economy today as it was then with its thousands of acres of groves, packinghouses, processing plants and even seasonal gift fruit shippers.

But the area offered other important agricultural and commercial opportunities as well. Farmsteads produced hearty crops of corn, tomatoes, potatoes, cabbages and beans. With many of the crops being exported to out-of-area markets a business community began to emerge with banks, service centers, lodging and even a local newspaper then called the Vero Press.

Increasing growth and development led to more much needed services, and the people's entrepreneurial spirit endeavored to meet the needs. Soon after there appeared a department store and drug store as well as a casino, several restaurants and a movie theater.

Growing modernization brought more and more industry to the area including Eastern Air Lines and Piper Aircraft, and with them came an influx of inhabitants looking to make Vero Beach their home. The unique charm and beauty of the area along with its miles of untouched gorgeous beaches were no longer secret to the outside world, and tourism emerged as another significant industry.

OPPOSITE: The Sweet Shop, a coffee shop owned by Bill and Marge Redman at 1327 21st Street, Vero Beach, 1958. Behind the counter, from left, are Marge, Bill, and their oldest daughter Judy. Seated are their younger children Donny, Jimmy, Beth, Kathy and Kerry. COURTESY BETH REDMAN KRAY

LEFT: Rows of corn at Indian River Farms, July 6, 1917.
COURTESY INDIAN RIVER PRESS JOURNAL

OPPOSITE TOP: Vero Press building, circa 1915.
COURTESY INDIAN RIVER PRESS JOURNAL

OPPOSITE BOTTOM LEFT: Five men work to unload crates of tomatoes at a packing house built by the Indian River Growers Association, circa 1910.
COURTESY INDIAN RIVER COUNTY HISTORICAL SOCIETY COLLECTION, ARCHIVE CENTER, INDIAN RIVER COUNTY MAIN LIBRARY

OPPOSITE BOTTOM RIGHT: Green bean yield from Indian River Farms, December 15, 1916. COURTESY INDIAN RIVER PRESS JOURNAL

ABOVE: Crates of winter-grown potatoes at Vero Potato Packing House, April 10, 1917.
COURTESY INDIAN RIVER PRESS JOURNAL

LEFT: Two-year-old grapefruit tree on Indian River Farms, circa 1917.
COURTESY INDIAN RIVER PRESS JOURNAL

OPPOSITE: Buckwheat field at Indian River Farms, circa 1917. COURTESY INDIAN RIVER PRESS JOURNAL

BELOW: Picking white wax beans at Indian River Farms, January 10, 1917.
COURTESY INDIAN RIVER PRESS JOURNAL

ABOVE: Early grove owner and workers, mule pulling trailer of wooden crates, circa 1915.
COURTESY INDIAN RIVER COUNTY HISTORICAL SOCIETY COLLECTION, ARCHIVE CENTER, INDIAN RIVER COUNTY MAIN LIBRARY

RIGHT: Herman Carlsward holding a potato plant on the farm at the Carlsward homestead, West Barber Avenue, Vero, 1919. COURTESY MARILYN CARLSWARD INGRAM

OPPOSITE TOP: Business section in Vero, including Maher's Department Store in its early years, circa 1920. COURTESY ARCHIVE CENTER, INDIAN RIVER COUNTY MAIN LIBRARY

OPPOSITE BOTTOM: Sleepy Eye Lodge, circa 1919. COURTESY INDIAN RIVER PRESS JOURNAL

ABOVE: The Fellsmere Inn, circa 1920s. The structure was built in 1911 by the Fellsmere Farms Company for visitors who came to buy land in Fellsmere. It was sold to Theodore Moore, Florida's "Pineapple King," and transformed by architect Frederick Trimble into the Broadway Inn. In the mid-1920s it was transformed back to the Fellsmere Inn. Realtor Fred Vandeveer bought the inn in 2005 and completely restored it to its former glory.
COURTESY CLARENCE F. "KORKY" KORKER

ABOVE RIGHT: Hardee Service Station, Sebastian. Corner of Main Street and Indian River Drive. Identifications: George F. Vickers (standing near front fender), S. O. Davis (sitting at base of post), L. F. Chesser (standing at doorway).
COURTESY INDIAN RIVER COUNTY HISTORICAL SOCIETY COLLECTION, ARCHIVE CENTER, INDIAN RIVER COUNTY MAIN LIBRARY

RIGHT: Formal opening of Barrett's Steak House between Vero Beach and Ft. Pierce, May 21, 1935. Standing to the right of the trombone player at center is Edward A. C. Elliot. COURTESY SHARON PIKE

OPPOSITE: Vero Beach Realty Board, February 21, 1929, outside Beachland Casino. Herman Zeuch of Indian River Farms is sitting and holding cane.
COURTESY INDIAN RIVER COUNTY HISTORICAL SOCIETY COLLECTION, ARCHIVE CENTER, INDIAN RIVER COUNTY MAIN LIBRARY

ABOVE: Workers involved in digging the Vero Beach canals, 1939. The group includes Alvin and Carl Carlsward. COURTESY MARILYN CARLSWARD INGRAM

ABOVE LEFT: Sign painter Carl A. Elliot showing off his handiwork at the Royal Park Inn, Vero Beach, circa 1930s. COURTESY SHARON PIKE

LEFT: Seven workers prepare to transfer a cargo of watermelons from truck to train car, circa 1940.
COURTESY INDIAN RIVER COUNTY HISTORICAL SOCIETY COLLECTION, ARCHIVE CENTER, INDIAN RIVER COUNTY MAIN LIBRARY

OPPOSITE: Workers pack fruit inside a packing house, April 28, 1937.
COURTESY INDIAN RIVER COUNTY HISTORICAL SOCIETY COLLECTION, ARCHIVE CENTER, INDIAN RIVER COUNTY MAIN LIBRARY

ABOVE: Earle B. Thatcher and Press Journal editor Harry S. Schultz stand next to a bus load of children in front of the Chamber of Commerce building in the early 1940s.
COURTESY INDIAN RIVER COUNTY HISTORICAL SOCIETY COLLECTION, ARCHIVE CENTER, INDIAN RIVER COUNTY MAIN LIBRARY

ABOVE RIGHT: A car that drove through the front display window of Wodtke's Department Store on 14th Avenue in downtown Vero Beach in 1943. COURTESY SUSAN WODTKE SMITH

RIGHT: The Osceola Pharmacy, on the corner of 14th Avenue and 20th Street, circa 1940s. The pharmacy was owned by Hennig-Myers families. Friedlander's, the Illinois Hotel, and Jun's Grocery and Market are also visible.
COURTESY INDIAN RIVER COUNTY HISTORICAL SOCIETY COLLECTION, ARCHIVE CENTER, INDIAN RIVER COUNTY MAIN LIBRARY

OPPOSITE: The Florida Theatre at night, circa 1940s.
COURTESY INDIAN RIVER COUNTY HISTORICAL SOCIETY COLLECTION, ARCHIVE CENTER, INDIAN RIVER COUNTY MAIN LIBRARY

ABOVE: Ayers & Kennedy Fruit Market in Vero Beach in the 1940s. COURTESY SMITH COLLECTION, ARCHIVE CENTER, INDIAN RIVER COUNTY MAIN LIBRARY

OPPOSITE TOP: Barker-Williams Air Conditioning, Barker Electric Company, and Williams Refrigeration Service, located at 1305 19th Place, circa 1940s. The businesses were owned by Q. Hans Barker and Ned L. Williams. COURTESY INDIAN RIVER COUNTY HISTORICAL SOCIETY COLLECTION, ARCHIVE CENTER, INDIAN RIVER COUNTY MAIN LIBRARY

OPPOSITE BOTTOM LEFT: Del Mar Hotel, circa 1940s. Markings on front:"Hotel Del Mar Vero Beach, Florida C-778" COURTESY INDIAN RIVER COUNTY HISTORICAL SOCIETY COLLECTION, ARCHIVE CENTER, INDIAN RIVER COUNTY MAIN LIBRARY

OPPOSITE BOTTOM RIGHT: An employee loads tomatoes into crates at the Hogan & Sons Packing House, circa 1940s. About 1,000 acres of Indian River County soil were planted with tomatoes in the fall and spring seasons. COURTESY INDIAN RIVER COUNTY HISTORICAL SOCIETY COLLECTION, ARCHIVE CENTER, INDIAN RIVER COUNTY MAIN LIBRARY

ABOVE: Fruit stand owned and operated by Joseph Bezzant Walker and his wife Ellen Walker at the northeast corner of Old Dixie Hwy. and 49th Street, circa 1949. COURTESY BRENDA CORUM

LEFT: Elizabeth Graves at the Driftwood Inn, Vero Beach, circa 1950s.
COURTESY SEXTON COLLECTION, ARCHIVE CENTER, INDIAN RIVER COUNTY MAIN LIBRARY

OPPOSITE TOP LEFT: Hawaiian Shop store front on Ocean Drive, Humiston Beach area in the mid-1950s. The shop's owner was Katharine "Kitty" Bailey-Willis. COURTESY JACKIE VITEK

OPPOSITE BOTTOM LEFT: Gulf service station in Vero Beach, late 1950s.
COURTESY INDIAN RIVER PRESS JOURNAL

OPPOSITE RIGHT: Elmer Arendas with his wife Stella and son Ronnie in front of the family's fruit stand on US 1 in South Vero, circa 1949.
COURTESY VALERIE L. ARENDAS

RIGHT: Driftwood Inn in the 1950s.

OPPOSITE: Jewel Palms Deluxe Motor Hotel and Coffee Shop on the intersection of Ocean Drive and Camelia Lane, circa 1955.

BELOW AND BELOW RIGHT: People eating at the homestead clubhouse of P.O. Clements, September, 1956. P. O. (Howard Lee) Clements Collection. Donated by Anne Clements Cabot. Markings on back: B717.

ABOVE: A group gathers for the dedication ceremony of the Howard Johnson Motel, located on 17th Street and US 1. From left: Jim Kressler, Anthony Gianotti, Marie Gianotti, Jack Sturgis, unknown, Merrill Barber, unknown, unknown, Norman Hensick.

COURTESY INDIAN RIVER COUNTY HISTORICAL SOCIETY COLLECTION, ARCHIVE CENTER, INDIAN RIVER COUNTY MAIN LIBRARY

ABOVE LEFT: Waldo Sexton at the original Driftwood Inn, circa 1960.

COURTESY SEXTON COLLECTION, ARCHIVE CENTER, INDIAN RIVER COUNTY MAIN LIBRARY

LEFT: Two employees of Hogan & Sons Packing House load a truck with crates of tomatoes, circa 1960s.

COURTESY INDIAN RIVER COUNTY HISTORICAL SOCIETY COLLECTION, ARCHIVE CENTER, INDIAN RIVER COUNTY MAIN LIBRARY

OPPOSITE: Interior of the Piper Aircraft plant, May 1961.

COURTESY INDIAN RIVER PRESS JOURNAL

ABOVE: A postcard view of Southgate Village, 1282 8th Avenue in Vero Beach, circa 1960s. The business advertised 85 modern, spacious mobile home locations plus shopping, churches, restaurants and fishing nearby. The business is still family owned and will be celebrating their 60th anniversary in 2016. COURTESY AJ WOLD

ABOVE RIGHT: Hamilton Grocery and Service Station at the corner of Old Dixie and 69th Street in Winter Beach, circa 1962. The business was owned by J.J.P. Hamilton, county commissioner for years. He and his wife lived in the two-story house beside the business. Across the road was a house and fruit stand owned by C.N. Anderson. COURTESY JANET ANDERSON

RIGHT: Interior of the Piper Aircraft plant, June 1962. COURTESY INDIAN RIVER PRESS JOURNAL

ABOVE: WTTB's 10th birthday celebration, 1964. COURTESY INDIAN RIVER PRESS JOURNAL

ABOVE RIGHT: Realtors Banquet, December 15, 1965. From left: unknown, Roy Neville behind mike, unknown, Jill Maher, Marguerite Schlitt.
COURTESY INDIAN RIVER COUNTY HISTORICAL SOCIETY COLLECTION, ARCHIVE CENTER, INDIAN RIVER COUNTY MAIN LIBRARY

RIGHT: Piper Aircraft electrics division, circa 1960s. COURTESY INDIAN RIVER PRESS JOURNAL

OPPOSITE: Florigold Citrus being packed at the Exchange Packers packing house, circa 1960s. Man in the picture was called Smitty.
COURTESY INDIAN RIVER COUNTY HISTORICAL SOCIETY COLLECTION, ARCHIVE CENTER, INDIAN RIVER COUNTY MAIN LIBRARY

ABOVE: Graders and packers at work inside the packing house at Indian River Packing Company in Gifford, circa 1960s. COURTESY JANET ANDERSON

ABOVE LEFT: Charlie Anderson at the rear of a truck loaded with Indian River Citrus, ready to go north, Indian River Packing Company, Gifford, circa 1966. COURTESY JANET ANDERSON

LEFT: Publix Market in Vero Beach, circa 1967. COURTESY INDIAN RIVER PRESS JOURNAL

OPPOSITE: Gulf Servicenter in the 1960s. COURTESY INDIAN RIVER PRESS JOURNAL

CHAPTER FIVE

COMMUNITY

Nothing reflects the spirit of a community like its people, and the communities of Indian River County, even before it was so named in 1925, are no different.

The pioneer spirit was by all accounts strong, as area ancestors adopted a rural existence that had them relying on themselves and their neighbors. It was this spirit of deep community that drew the people together in both work and play. They pooled their time and energy to dig canals, build roads, bridges, churches and schools, and even fight storms.

From the early days it became apparent that civic duty and volunteerism was an essential ingredient not only for survival, but for socialization also. Much of that spirit, comradery and pride can still be found today.

OPPOSITE: Members of the Aladdin Club enjoy a group luncheon on May 15, 1923.
COURTESY INDIAN RIVER COUNTY HISTORICAL SOCIETY COLLECTION, ARCHIVE CENTER, INDIAN RIVER COUNTY MAIN LIBRARY

ABOVE: 19 automobile loads of prospective land buyers assembling at Sleepy Eye Lodge before touring Indian River Farms, February 9, 1917.
COURTESY INDIAN RIVER PRESS JOURNAL

LEFT: Entrance to McKee Jungle Gardens, circa 1932.
COURTESY MCKEE BOTANICAL GARDEN ARCHIVES

OPPOSITE TOP LEFT: Anna Orth before she was married, early 1900s.
COURTESY LYNN LYSNE WILLIAMS

OPPOSITE TOP RIGHT: Osceola Apartments, circa 1930s.
COURTESY INDIAN RIVER PRESS JOURNAL

OPPOSITE BOTTOM: Prospective land buyers touring the Walker Grove at Indian River Farms, February 9, 1917. COURTESY INDIAN RIVER PRESS JOURNAL

ABOVE: A young woman holds an exotic Pelican flower (*Aristolochia grandiflora*) at McKee Jungle Gardens, circa 1930s. COURTESY MCKEE BOTANICAL GARDEN ARCHIVES

RIGHT: Mahogany slab table purchased by Waldo Sexton at NYC Worlds Fair in 1939 for the Hall of Giants at McKee Botanical Garden. COURTESY SEXTON COLLECTION, ARCHIVE CENTER, INDIAN RIVER COUNTY MAIN LIBRARY

ABOVE: Vero Beach Beautification Day workers, circa 1930s. COURTESY INDIAN RIVER PRESS JOURNAL

LEFT: Bill Wodtke Sr. and his wife Edna with Bill Wodtke Jr., left, and Catherine "Kay" Wodtke in 1935. The couple would open Wodtke's Department Store in 1942. The store served the area for 57 years. COURTESY SUSAN WODTKE SMITH

ABOVE: Tom Howell with whale bones, McKee Jungle Gardens, circa 1950.

COURTESY SEXTON COLLECTION, ARCHIVE CENTER, INDIAN RIVER COUNTY MAIN LIBRARY

ABOVE RIGHT: Ronnie and Gary Arendas, sons of Elmer and Stella, in front of the family's fruit and souvenir stand on US 1 in South Vero, circa 1949. COURTESY VALERIE L. ARENDAS

RIGHT: From left, Shirley Heilman (Ostrander), Roger Heilman, Ernie Smallman, Don Heilman, Jim Heilman, and Betty Heilman Szalkowski at Circle Trailer Park in Vero Beach, 1949. COURTESY SHIRLEY HEILMAN OSTRANDER

OPPOSITE: High water from Hurricane Jenny, October 18. 1950.

COURTESY INDIAN RIVER PRESS JOURNAL

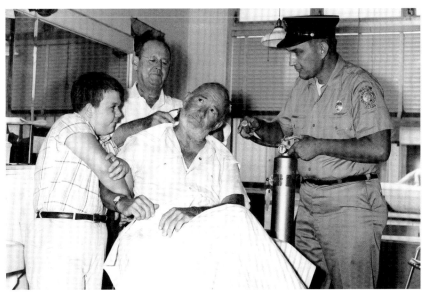

ABOVE: Mrs. Waddell with a Brownie Troop. Front row, from left: Debbie Howard, Ann Kelso, Sue Schlitt. Second row: Anita Hatshbarger, Sandra Waddell, Patty Skiscim, Sue Wodtke, Kitty Waddell. Third row: Anita Marie Smith, Ramona Smith, Lynn Hart, Betty Schlitt, Delys Mullis. Back row: Henderson, Susan Helseth, Becky Scher, Claudia Kennis.
COURTESY WADDELL COLLECTION, ARCHIVE CENTER, INDIAN RIVER COUNTY MAIN LIBRARY

ABOVE LEFT: Girl Scouts and clown Emmett Kelly pause for a photo in downtown Vero Beach circa 1955. COURTESY INDIAN RIVER COUNTY HISTORICAL SOCIETY COLLECTION, ARCHIVE CENTER, INDIAN RIVER COUNTY MAIN LIBRARY

LEFT: P. O. Clements, airport manager, getting his beard trimmed by Al Herndon, with son Paul watching. Local firefighter standing by with fire extinguisher.
COURTESY INDIAN RIVER COUNTY HISTORICAL SOCIETY COLLECTION, ARCHIVE CENTER, INDIAN RIVER COUNTY MAIN LIBRARY

OPPOSITE: Installation of Vero Beach Junior Woman's Club officers for 1955-1956. From left: Mardella Sutherland, Rose Anne Dancy, incoming president Patsy Helseth, outgoing president Sara Chesnutt, Jean Gould, Louise Cavender, Senior Woman's Club chaperone Mrs. Fitz.
COURTESY PATSY E. HELSETH

ABOVE: Elmer Arendas and his father-in-law Matthew Judge Owoc in front of a fruit and souvenir stand in South Vero, circa 1958.

COURTESY VALERIE L. ARENDAS

RIGHT: First Baptist Church cornerstone ceremony, November 1961.

COURTESY INDIAN RIVER PRESS JOURNAL

OPPOSITE: First Baptist Church groundbreaking ceremony, April 1961.

COURTESY INDIAN RIVER PRESS JOURNAL

ABOVE: Meeting of the Epsilon ETA, BSP, in Vero Beach, circa 1969. Beta Sigma Phi started in Vero in 1955 by invitation only and is still active. Seated from left are: Mrs. Robert Orton, Mrs. Nick Ryan, Mrs. Robert Mooney, Mrs. Peter E. Peck, Mrs. James Pomar. Standing from left: Mrs. John Gallagher, Mrs. Karl Watson, Mrs. Darrell Ellis, Mrs. Gordon Trimmer, Mrs. Sam Holcomb, and Mrs. William French. COURTESY RUBY WALKER

LEFT: Mrs. S.B. Taylor participating in the Presbyterian Church groundbreaking ceremony, February 1960.
COURTESY INDIAN RIVER PRESS JOURNAL

OPPOSITE: Inside the Hall of Giants is a priceless artifact - a table made of the single largest plank of mahogany wood, measuring 35 feet long and 5 feet wide. It is still on display today at McKee Botanical Garden. COURTESY MCKEE BOTANICAL GARDEN ARCHIVES

ABOVE: Vero Beach Dolphinettes, January 1961. The Dolphinettes were a highly competitive, amateur water ballet group founded in 1951 by Mildred Frasier (Bunnell). This synchronized swimming group was made up of teenage girls from Vero Beach High School. They practiced primarily in the large pool at the Windswept (Southward Inn) Hotel in Vero Beach and performed at local pools and at locations throughout the state, which included the Palm Beach Biltmore, the Bahama Club (Melbourne), Silver Springs, and Cypress Gardens. After witnessing the positive publicity the Dolphinettes brought to Vero Beach and Indian River County, both the Chamber of Commerce and the Beach Business Bureau contributed to their travel and expense fund. COURTESY INDIAN RIVER PRESS JOURNAL

RIGHT: A group of kids in front of Katharine (Kitty) Bailey-Willis' house on Route 60/Osceola. From left: Thomas "Tommy" Selby Lowther, Dede Garrison, Dusty Garrison, Maurice "Gus" Lowther, Joseph "Joe" Daniel Lowther, Jr. COURTESY JACKIE VITEK

ABOVE: Dining at he Vero Beach Yacht Club in the 1960s are, from left: Joseph "Joe" Daniel Lowther, Jr., Joseph "Joe" Daniel Lowther, Sr., Thomas "Tommy" Selby Lowther, Jacqueline Bebe Willis-Lowther, Maurice "Gus" Lowther.

COURTESY JACKIE VITEK

LEFT: Merrill P. Barber shakes hands with youngster in uniform, circa 1969.

COURTESY INDIAN RIVER COUNTY HISTORICAL SOCIETY COLLECTION, ARCHIVE CENTER, INDIAN RIVER COUNTY MAIN LIBRARY

CHAPTER SIX

PUBLIC SERVICE

The public must be served and from the very beginning, it has been by the region's firefighters, law enforcement officers, doctors, nurses, school teachers, bankers, state, city and town and village officials and so many others.

The Indian River Historical Society has hundreds of photographs of selected officials, police officers, firefighters, court officials, post office workers and others doing their jobs, serving the community. Many of which are included in this chapter.

Proudly, this chapter also includes photos of US Navy Officers, Airmen and even WAVES that served our nation at the Naval Air Station during World War II. The war years led to many changes in the area including a much expanded and improved municipal airport and thousands of new residents, as many of the 1,400 servicemen and women returned to Vero Beach to make it their new home.

OPPOSITE: Six firemen and their five vehicles in front of the Vero Beach Fire Department, circa 1948. The police station is visible to the left.
COURTESY INDIAN RIVER COUNTY HISTORICAL SOCIETY COLLECTION, ARCHIVE CENTER, INDIAN RIVER COUNTY MAIN LIBRARY

ABOVE: U.S. Army drill team on Seminole Avenue (14th Avenue), prior to WWI, circa 1916. Donated by Rebecca Rodenberg.
COURTESY INDIAN RIVER COUNTY HISTORICAL SOCIETY COLLECTION, ARCHIVE CENTER, INDIAN RIVER COUNTY MAIN LIBRARY

ABOVE RIGHT: The first fire station in Vero Beach, circa 1928. The station was located on the northeast corner of 13th Avenue and Osceola Blvd (20th Street). The volunteer force is in full attire. Included in photo are Paul Beindorf, Charlie Tool, Harold Redstone, and Slim Stansberry. COURTESY INDIAN RIVER COUNTY HISTORICAL SOCIETY COLLECTION, ARCHIVE CENTER, INDIAN RIVER COUNTY MAIN LIBRARY

RIGHT: Local air mail is loaded onto an Eastern Air Lines mail plane at Vero Beach Airport circa 1940s. From left: Charles Morris, pilot; B.H. Lockett, Assistant Superintendent of Airmail Service in Atlanta; George Gardner, Operations Manager of Eastern Air Lines; P.O. (Howard Lee) Clements, Dispatcher; B. L. Holman, Manager of the Airport; and John Schumann, Vero Beach Postmaster. An unidentified woman stands to the right of the airplane door.
COURTESY INDIAN RIVER COUNTY HISTORICAL SOCIETY COLLECTION, ARCHIVE CENTER, INDIAN RIVER COUNTY MAIN LIBRARY

OPPOSITE: The boardwalk and lifeguard station at Humiston Park, circa 1960s. COURTESY INDIAN RIVER COUNTY HISTORICAL SOCIETY COLLECTION, ARCHIVE CENTER, INDIAN RIVER COUNTY MAIN LIBRARY

ABOVE: Girl Scout troop with Betty Earman (Mrs. Joe S. Earman) touring NAS Vero Beach, May 24, 1943. Naval officer/tour guide standing behind Betty Earman.
COURTESY INDIAN RIVER COUNTY HISTORICAL SOCIETY COLLECTION, ARCHIVE CENTER, INDIAN RIVER COUNTY MAIN LIBRARY

ABOVE LEFT: WAVE officers at NAS Vero Beach during WWII.
COURTESY INDIAN RIVER COUNTY HISTORICAL SOCIETY COLLECTION, ARCHIVE CENTER, INDIAN RIVER COUNTY MAIN LIBRARY

LEFT: War Bond Parade, June 2, 1943, NAS Vero Beach and WWII.
COURTESY INDIAN RIVER COUNTY HISTORICAL SOCIETY COLLECTION, ARCHIVE CENTER, INDIAN RIVER COUNTY MAIN LIBRARY

OPPOSITE: Alex MacWilliam, a WWI veteran, leads the 1941 Armistice Day Parade through Vero Beach. The Vero Beach High School Band follows behind.
COURTESY INDIAN RIVER COUNTY HISTORICAL SOCIETY COLLECTION, ARCHIVE CENTER, INDIAN RIVER COUNTY MAIN LIBRARY

ABOVE: WAVES third anniversary celebration at Hall of Giants.
COURTESY INDIAN RIVER COUNTY HISTORICAL SOCIETY COLLECTION, ARCHIVE CENTER,
INDIAN RIVER COUNTY MAIN LIBRARY

ABOVE RIGHT: WAVES at attention while on the paved parking
area adjacent to the Beachland Hotel (barracks), 1945.
COURTESY INDIAN RIVER COUNTY HISTORICAL SOCIETY COLLECTION, ARCHIVE CENTER,
INDIAN RIVER COUNTY MAIN LIBRARY

RIGHT: Sig and Gwenn Lysne at Vero Beach, 1944. Sig flew Hellcats off
the U.S.S. Hancock in the Pacific during WWII, logging more than 70
flights with hits to two Japanese planes. Sig and his brother-in-law Kinky
Orth later established the Indian River Flying Service in 1946. The two
men were crop dusters and FAA instructors for more than 40 years.
COURTESY LYNN LYSNE WILLIAMS

ABOVE: Responder vehicles in front of the Vero Beach Fire Department and Police Station, circa 1950s.
COURTESY INDIAN RIVER COUNTY HISTORICAL SOCIETY COLLECTION, ARCHIVE CENTER, INDIAN RIVER COUNTY MAIN LIBRARY

LEFT: Collection of photographs of unidentified U.S. Navy WAVE who served at NAS Vero Beach, during WWII, 1943-1946. Markings on front: "Halloween Party."
COURTESY INDIAN RIVER COUNTY HISTORICAL SOCIETY COLLECTION, ARCHIVE CENTER, INDIAN RIVER COUNTY MAIN LIBRARY

ABOVE: City Hall in Vero Beach, circa 1948. COURTESY SMITH COLLECTION, ARCHIVE CENTER, INDIAN RIVER COUNTY MAIN LIBRARY

LEFT: Comdr. Herbert MacIntosh and Ensign Jean Ott, wedding guests arriving at Community Church. L. to R.: Capt. Robert Worrack, Lt. Comdr. Boyd Mewburn, Mrs. Ella Worrack, Mrs. Hazel Mewburn. March 23, 1946. COURTESY INDIAN RIVER COUNTY HISTORICAL SOCIETY COLLECTION, ARCHIVE CENTER, INDIAN RIVER COUNTY MAIN LIBRARY

OPPOSITE: Men prepare for the Fire Station's groundbreaking ceremony, circa 1950.
From left: Monk Baughman, Charles Toole, James Barrett, Larry Maher, Jr., Paul Beindorf.
COURTESY INDIAN RIVER COUNTY HISTORICAL SOCIETY COLLECTION, ARCHIVE CENTER, INDIAN RIVER COUNTY MAIN LIBRARY

ABOVE: Twenty-three American Red Cross nurses sit for a photograph at the Vero Beach Red Cross Building, circa 1955.
COURTESY INDIAN RIVER COUNTY HISTORICAL SOCIETY COLLECTION, ARCHIVE CENTER, INDIAN RIVER COUNTY MAIN LIBRARY

ABOVE RIGHT: Indian River County law enforcement in the 1950s. P. O. Clements, deputy sheriff, back row, far right. Also identified: Jesse Selph (front row, 3rd from left) and John Wakenka (back row, 3rd from left).
COURTESY INDIAN RIVER COUNTY HISTORICAL SOCIETY COLLECTION, ARCHIVE CENTER, INDIAN RIVER COUNTY MAIN LIBRARY

RIGHT: Vero Beach Fire Department, Station No. 1, with firemen, circa 1950s. Fire Chief Guy Sullivan is on the far right, wearing a white cap.
COURTESY INDIAN RIVER COUNTY HISTORICAL SOCIETY COLLECTION, ARCHIVE CENTER, INDIAN RIVER COUNTY MAIN LIBRARY

OPPOSITE: A group gather for the groundbreaking and dedication ceremony for the new American Red Cross building in 1957. From left: Dorothy Wimbrow, Augusta Conn, Earl Sappington, Mary Lou Durrance, Merrill P. Barber, Gov. Leroy Collins, Roswell Mower, Millie C. Bunnell, Joe Henry Earman, and one unidentified man.
COURTESY INDIAN RIVER COUNTY HISTORICAL SOCIETY COLLECTION, ARCHIVE CENTER, INDIAN RIVER COUNTY MAIN LIBRARY

ABOVE: Vero Beach Fire Department ladder truck, March 1961 COURTESY INDIAN RIVER PRESS JOURNAL

LEFT: Vero Beach Police Department, circa 1960.
COURTESY INDIAN RIVER PRESS JOURNAL

OPPOSITE: An NCO watches two privates hose down an upended trailer cart. Two Jeeps and several 1950s automobiles can be seen in the background.
COURTESY INDIAN RIVER COUNTY HISTORICAL SOCIETY COLLECTION, ARCHIVE CENTER, INDIAN RIVER COUNTY MAIN LIBRARY

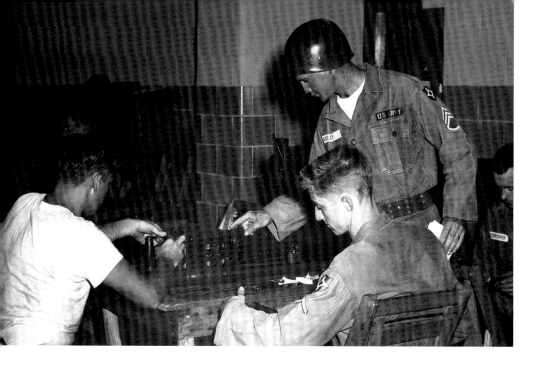

ABOVE: An NCO (wearing helmet) stands beside two privates seated at a table with an automatic weapon, circa 1965. The NCO points to a feature of the weapon while one trainee holds it.

COURTESY INDIAN RIVER COUNTY HISTORICAL SOCIETY COLLECTION, ARCHIVE CENTER, INDIAN RIVER COUNTY MAIN LIBRARY

ABOVE RIGHT: Head lifeguard Charles Gollnick (front row, first from left) with five assistants at Sexton Plaza beach, circa 1960s.

COURTESY INDIAN RIVER COUNTY HISTORICAL SOCIETY COLLECTION, ARCHIVE CENTER, INDIAN RIVER COUNTY MAIN LIBRARY

RIGHT: Jim Pease of the Vero Beach Sheriff's Department (right) checking with John Harrington and Tom Hodges following a fender bender, May 1960.

COURTESY INDIAN RIVER PRESS JOURNAL

OPPOSITE: Vero Beach Fire Department vehicles, October 1967.

COURTESY INDIAN RIVER PRESS JOURNAL

CHAPTER SEVEN

RECREATION

When many of the Navy men and women relocated to Vero Beach and surrounding areas after World War II, it was said that one of the things that attracted them to the area was its year-round warm climate; its untouched beaches where they could relax and play; the beautiful Indian River Lagoon where they could fish from sunrise to sunset and the friendly people.

Recreational places are important to a region and Indian River County is blessed with many such places throughout. Following the war, the area was blessed even further when the Brooklyn Dodgers chose Vero Beach as their spring training home, bringing one of America's favorite pastimes to the region.

Photos in this chapter show men, women and youngsters enjoying this "year round vacationland" and taking advantage of the many recreational opportunities in Indian River County. From enjoying a day at Waldo Sexton's Jungle Gardens, to catching a ballgame at Holman Stadium, to boating, fishing, golfing, swimming, tennis and much more.

OPPOSITE: Dodgers players with Vero beauties and Indian River oranges at Holman Stadium, circa 1950s.
COURTESY INDIAN RIVER COUNTY HISTORICAL SOCIETY COLLECTION, ARCHIVE CENTER, INDIAN RIVER COUNTY MAIN LIBRARY

ABOVE: Beachgoers, December 1914.

RIGHT: Arthur Schoessel admires a admires a bear, named Alice, at the Pocahontas Park Zoo, Vero, circa 1920s.

OPPOSITE TOP: Vero winter-time bathers, circa 1917.

OPPOSITE BOTTOM LEFT: Wabasso church picnic, circa 1910, held near the E. E. Smith home. Included in the photo are John E. Jamison, Catherine Lasker and Katherine G. Jamison.

OPPOSITE BOTTOM RIGHT: Young tennis players, circa 1926. Dorothy Henning and Mamie Leffler are among those pictured.

ABOVE: A golfer holding his club waits beside the tee box as his companion finishes his drive on the Riomar Golf Course in the 1920s. Incorporated in 1925, Riomar is the oldest club in Indian River County and one of the oldest in the state. When the first nine holes were completed in 1919, it was the only golf course between Daytona and Palm Beach. COURTESY HILL COLLECTION, ARCHIVE CENTER, INDIAN RIVER COUNTY MAIN LIBRARY

LEFT: Members of Vero's Basketball Team in the 1920s. From left: Tip Rice, Peters, Sonny Horn, Russ Applegate, Walter Shelton. COURTESY INDIAN RIVER COUNTY HISTORICAL SOCIETY COLLECTION, ARCHIVE CENTER, INDIAN RIVER COUNTY MAIN LIBRARY

OPPOSITE: Canoeing at McKee Jungle Gardens, circa 1935. COURTESY SEXTON COLLECTION, ARCHIVE CENTER, INDIAN RIVER COUNTY MAIN LIBRARY

ABOVE: Jean Frost, Cookie Smith, Jean Gifford, Thelma Simmons, and Margaret Bazler enjoy the beach in the late 1940s.
COURTESY INDIAN RIVER COUNTY HISTORICAL SOCIETY COLLECTION, ARCHIVE CENTER, INDIAN RIVER COUNTY MAIN LIBRARY

ABOVE RIGHT: Six women on the high and low diving boards at Beachland Pool in the early 1940s. From left: Ruth Hilliard, Jean Gifford, Alice Smith, Margaret Bazler, Thelma Simmons, Jean Frost.
COURTESY INDIAN RIVER COUNTY HISTORICAL SOCIETY COLLECTION, ARCHIVE CENTER, INDIAN RIVER COUNTY MAIN LIBRARY

BELOW RIGHT: Earle G. Thatcher (Chamber Secretary, 3rd from right) and nine other passengers on a fishing trip aboard the KATHLEEN, May 27, 1936.
COURTESY INDIAN RIVER COUNTY HISTORICAL SOCIETY COLLECTION, ARCHIVE CENTER, INDIAN RIVER COUNTY MAIN LIBRARY

OPPOSITE: McKee Jungle Gardens cofounder Waldo Sexton with one of its most well known attractions, spider monkeys, in the late 1930s.
COURTESY SEXTON COLLECTION, ARCHIVE CENTER, INDIAN RIVER COUNTY MAIN LIBRARY

ABOVE: Supporters of the Vero Beach Dodgers on their way to the 1949 World Series. On steps: C. McClure, Miles Warren, Bud Holman, John Schuman Jr., John Schuman Sr., Harold Elliott, Larry Maher Jr., Bump Holman. Front row: Luster Merriman, Dorabelle Holman, Fred Briggs, Jack Howard, Charles Toole, Jim Barrett, Allison Warren.
COURTESY INDIAN RIVER COUNTY HISTORICAL SOCIETY COLLECTION, ARCHIVE CENTER, INDIAN RIVER COUNTY MAIN LIBRARY

ABOVE RIGHT: In 1948, Dodgertown, Vero Beach became the first integrated Major League Baseball Spring Training site in the South, where African-American Dodgers stayed on base, dined and recreated together. In March 1950, (L-R) Hall of Fame catcher Roy Campanella, pitcher Don Newcombe, pitcher Dan Bankhead and Hall of Fame infielder Jackie Robinson, who broke baseball's color line, gather at Dodgertown. Newcombe won Rookie of the Year, Cy Young and MVP awards, while Bankhead was the first African-American pitcher in the major leagues. Photo taken by Peter O'Malley, President, Los Angeles Dodgers, 1970-1998.
COURTESY BRADY BALLARD (HISTORIC DODGERTOWN) / PETER O'MALLEY, PRESIDENT, LOS ANGELES DODGERS, 1970-1998

RIGHT: Tuxedo Feeds baseball team with sponsor and coaches. Merrill P. Barber in suit and hat, James Barrett kneeling 2nd from left, others unidentified.
COURTESY INDIAN RIVER COUNTY HISTORICAL SOCIETY COLLECTION, ARCHIVE CENTER, INDIAN RIVER COUNTY MAIN LIBRARY

OPPOSITE: The historic Hall of Giants in the 1940s. This building was fully restored and may still be visited today. COURTESY MCKEE BOTANICAL GARDEN ARCHIVES

ABOVE: Press Journal fishing columnist Robert A. Dahne at the south jetty, Sebastian Inlet, 1949. COURTESY INDIAN RIVER PRESS JOURNAL

ABOVE LEFT: Two women pose with an impressive catch of fish for the Sportsmans Fishing Tournament at Vero Beach. The photo was used to promote tourism in the 1950s.
COURTESY INDIAN RIVER COUNTY HISTORICAL SOCIETY COLLECTION, ARCHIVE CENTER, INDIAN RIVER COUNTY MAIN LIBRARY

LEFT: Duck hunters displaying their trophies, circa 1950. From left: Kit Johnson, owner of Florida Sporting Goods Co.; Elmer Harris, Horace Gifford.
COURTESY INDIAN RIVER COUNTY HISTORICAL SOCIETY COLLECTION, ARCHIVE CENTER, INDIAN RIVER COUNTY MAIN LIBRARY

OPPOSITE: Sunbathing at the beach at Sexton Plaza, circa 1950s.
COURTESY INDIAN RIVER COUNTY HISTORICAL SOCIETY COLLECTION, ARCHIVE CENTER, INDIAN RIVER COUNTY MAIN LIBRARY

ABOVE: A crowd watching a Dodgers game at Holman Stadium on March 17, 1952. Don Vickers (far left, looking towards photographer) is among those in attendance.
COURTESY INDIAN RIVER COUNTY HISTORICAL SOCIETY COLLECTION, ARCHIVE CENTER, INDIAN RIVER COUNTY MAIN LIBRARY

RIGHT: As a teenager in 1951, Peter O'Malley, left, receives a warm greeting from Brooklyn Dodger shortstop and team captain Pee Wee Reese. In 1962, O'Malley became Director of Dodgertown. From 1970-1998 he was president of the Los Angeles Dodgers. The Dodgers held Spring Training at Dodgertown from 1948-2008. Reese was inducted into the National Baseball Hall of Fame in 1984. COURTESY BRENT SHYER

ABOVE: Brooklyn Dodgers President Walter O'Malley, left, and Bud Holman shake hands at dedication ceremonies for Holman Stadium on March 11, 1953. As an astute local community leader, Holman saw and acted on the opportunity to bring the Dodgers to Vero Beach for Spring Training. The plaque presented by the Dodgers reads, "The Brooklyn Dodgers Dedicate Holman Stadium to Honor Bud L. Holman of the Friendly City of Vero Beach, Walter F. O'Malley, President, Emil H. Praeger, C.E., Designer, 1953." COURTESY PETER O'MALLEY, PRESIDENT, LOS ANGELES DODGERS, 1970-1998 / BRADY BALLARD

LEFT: Indian River Citrus Bank baseball team. Adults standing, from left: Don Aulick, Ralph Harris, Merrill Barber. COURTESY INDIAN RIVER COUNTY HISTORICAL SOCIETY COLLECTION, ARCHIVE CENTER, INDIAN RIVER COUNTY MAIN LIBRARY

DODGERTOWN SUMMER CAMP
FOR BOYS AGES 10-16
JULY 1st TO AUGUST 25th

VERO BEACH

YEAR ROUND VACATION-LAND

Winter Home of
BROOKLYN DODGERS!
and affiliated Teams

'55 WORLD CHAMPS

ELLIOTT SIGN CO.

ABOVE: Dodgertown cafeteria in the 1950s.
COURTESY INDIAN RIVER COUNTY HISTORICAL SOCIETY COLLECTION, ARCHIVE CENTER, INDIAN RIVER COUNTY MAIN LIBRARY

ABOVE LEFT: Governor Leroy Collins stands at bat beside Dodger President Walter O'Malley, local business leader Bud Holman, and Florida State Senator Merrill Barber during a Dodger exhibition game, circa 1955.
COURTESY INDIAN RIVER COUNTY HISTORICAL SOCIETY COLLECTION, ARCHIVE CENTER, INDIAN RIVER COUNTY MAIN LIBRARY

LEFT: The Brooklyn Dodgers, winner of the 1955 World Series, sit on the berm at Holman Stadium in Vero Beach. Manager Walt Alston is kneeling on the bottom right.
COURTESY INDIAN RIVER COUNTY HISTORICAL SOCIETY COLLECTION, ARCHIVE CENTER, INDIAN RIVER COUNTY MAIN LIBRARY

OPPOSITE: The euphoria of the Dodgers winning the 1955 World Championship was also enjoyed in Vero Beach as the faithful arrived at spring training to see this billboard in 1956. In an exciting World Series, the Dodgers shut out the New York Yankees, 2-0, in Game 7 to capture the championship, the first and only one in Brooklyn. After training in Vero Beach, the 1956 Dodgers won the National League Pennant for the fourth time in five seasons. COURTESY BRADY BALLARD (HISTORIC DODGERTOWN)

ABOVE: Mr. and Mrs. Tate Simpson and their son enjoy the beach, circa 1950s.

ABOVE RIGHT: A hotel guest sunbathes on a diving board while others relax around the pool's edge, circa 1960.

RIGHT: Thirteen teenage Dolphinettes in dark swimsuits stand pool side by a diving board and sign reading "Year Round Vacationland: Vero Beach", circa 1960.

OPPOSITE: Eight artists paint and draw during an outing of the Vero Beach Art Club Inc., circa 1957.

ABOVE: Eight "palmetto" polo players on horseback pause for a photo, circa 1957.

COURTESY INDIAN RIVER COUNTY HISTORICAL SOCIETY COLLECTION, ARCHIVE CENTER, INDIAN RIVER COUNTY MAIN LIBRARY

RIGHT: Men and women enjoy a game of shuffleboard at Pocahontas Park, circa 1960.

COURTESY INDIAN RIVER COUNTY HISTORICAL SOCIETY COLLECTION, ARCHIVE CENTER, INDIAN RIVER COUNTY MAIN LIBRARY

OPPOSITE: Fishing from Wabasso Bridge, circa 1950s.

COURTESY INDIAN RIVER COUNTY HISTORICAL SOCIETY COLLECTION, ARCHIVE CENTER, INDIAN RIVER COUNTY MAIN LIBRARY

ABOVE: First Federal division champion Little League team, 1962. Bottom row: Stevie Smith, Timmy Graul, Jeff Flannery, Ricky Mishaw; 2nd row: Ricky Moore, Robert Mills, Jack LaBay, Henry Block, Ellis Green, Danny Sherwood; 3rd row: Eddie Widener, Gary Sanchez, Mark Clements, Ronny Brannan, Carl Fetzer. Manager Eddie Pfund
COURTESY INDIAN RIVER PRESS JOURNAL

ABOVE LEFT: Opening ceremonies for Vero Beach Little League Baseball, March 27, 1962. From left: John Struder, local Little League Baseball President; Jack Sturgis, Vero Beach Mayor; Peter O'Malley, in his first year as Director of Dodgertown; Don Drysdale, Dodger Hall of Fame pitcher; Lee Walls, Dodger outfielder. COURTESY BRENT SHYER

LEFT: On November 7, 1961, Director of Dodgertown Peter O'Malley, left, meets with Commissioner P. Scott Linder, of the Florida Development Commission, center, and Judge L.M. Merriman, Dodger attorney in Vero Beach. Linder was sent from Tallahassee by Florida Governor Farris Bryant to the Vero Beach City Council meeting. Linder's message stressed the significance and impact of keeping professional baseball teams training in Florida and, specifically, the Dodgers in Vero Beach. The Council and the Dodgers were in a dispute regarding the 1948 Airport Lease, but their differences were resolved. COURTESY BRENT SHYER

OPPOSITE: P. O. Clements and the "Fool's Den" musical group in the 1960s.
COURTESY INDIAN RIVER COUNTY HISTORICAL SOCIETY COLLECTION, ARCHIVE CENTER, INDIAN RIVER COUNTY MAIN LIBRARY

ABOVE: Pine car derby at Sea Scout building. From left: Mike Skiscum, Richard Schlitt, Billy Ausiello, Kim Hubbard.

COURTESY INDIAN RIVER PRESS JOURNAL

ABOVE RIGHT: The hula hoop craze hits Vero Beach in the 1960s.

COURTESY INDIAN RIVER COUNTY HISTORICAL SOCIETY COLLECTION, ARCHIVE CENTER, INDIAN RIVER COUNTY MAIN LIBRARY

RIGHT: Ten young ballet dancers from Maryan Carlson Dance Studio. Cathy Maher Williams is on the far right.

COURTESY INDIAN RIVER COUNTY HISTORICAL SOCIETY COLLECTION, ARCHIVE CENTER, INDIAN RIVER COUNTY MAIN LIBRARY

LEFT: Vero Beach Dolphinettes, circa 1960s. COURTESY INDIAN RIVER PRESS JOURNAL

CHAPTER EIGHT

CELEBRATION

Celebrations like anniversaries, weddings and parades punctuate the passage of time and allow for a deeper appreciation of our common history.

Often indistinguishable, recreation and celebration have long been a staple of the Vero lifestyle as these photos illustrate. Despite the old black-and-white images, it's almost as if color has transcended these pages because of the joyous festivities and merriment. You can almost envisage patriotic red, white and blue in the July 4th bunting, the trombone sparkling with its high gloss finish in the marching band or the bright citrus colors on the Indian River Fruit parade float.

Community celebrations whether they be ribbon-cuttings, festivals, sporting events, dances or troops returning home — any reason for a community to gather is cause for celebration.

OPPOSITE: Local beauties and dignitaries celebrate the dedication of Jaycee Park on March 22, 1958. Included are Edgar Schlitt, Governor Leroy Collins, Dolphinettes, unknown, and Merrill P. Barber. COURTESY INDIAN RIVER COUNTY HISTORICAL SOCIETY COLLECTION, ARCHIVE CENTER, INDIAN RIVER COUNTY MAIN LIBRARY

ABOVE: Anniversary celebration at the Vero Woman's Club, 1916.
COURTESY YOUNG COLLECTION, ARCHIVE CENTER, INDIAN RIVER COUNTY MAIN LIBRARY

RIGHT: Vero Woman's Club celebrating an anniversary in 1916. This view is of 21st Street and 16th Avenue (Mohawk Avenue) with the First Baptist Church in the background.
COURTESY INDIAN RIVER COUNTY HISTORICAL SOCIETY COLLECTION, ARCHIVE CENTER, INDIAN RIVER COUNTY MAIN LIBRARY

ABOVE: Another view of the anniversary celebration in Vero, 1916.

COURTESY INDIAN RIVER PRESS JOURNAL

LEFT: A crowd gathers around decorated cars parked in front of the Vero Theatre and Seminole Building, circa 1920s.

COURTESY INDIAN RIVER COUNTY HISTORICAL SOCIETY COLLECTION, ARCHIVE CENTER, INDIAN RIVER COUNTY MAIN LIBRARY

ABOVE: Children's parade down 20th Street, Vero Beach, circa 1940s.

COURTESY INDIAN RIVER PRESS JOURNAL

RIGHT: Ed Netto (wearing an American Legion cap) and two others prepare food at Pocahontas Park on Armistice Day, November 11, 1946.

COURTESY INDIAN RIVER COUNTY HISTORICAL SOCIETY COLLECTION, ARCHIVE CENTER,
INDIAN RIVER COUNTY MAIN LIBRARY

ABOVE: A crowd watches the Fourth of July Parade in downtown Vero Beach at the intersection of 20th Street and 14th Avenue, circa 1940s. Citrus Bank, Western Union, and the Florida Theatre are among the visible businesses. COURTESY INDIAN RIVER COUNTY HISTORICAL SOCIETY COLLECTION, ARCHIVE CENTER, INDIAN RIVER COUNTY MAIN LIBRARY

ABOVE LEFT: Armistice Day at the Heritage Community Center, 1948. COURTESY INDIAN RIVER PRESS JOURNAL

LEFT: Dedication ceremony at MacWilliam Park and the Charles Mitchell Highway on May 30, 1952. Included in picture are Gov. Fuller Warren, Lou Berger, W. D. Graves, Charles Heath, and Merrill Barber. COURTESY INDIAN RIVER COUNTY HISTORICAL SOCIETY COLLECTION, ARCHIVE CENTER, INDIAN RIVER COUNTY MAIN LIBRARY

ABOVE: Miss Labor Day Queen, August 30, 1968. COURTESY INDIAN RIVER PRESS JOURNAL

ABOVE LEFT: Vero Beach High School band at Waldo Sexton Day celebration, November 1958. COURTESY SEXTON COLLECTION, ARCHIVE CENTER, INDIAN RIVER COUNTY MAIN LIBRARY

LEFT: Santa Claus makes an appearance during Waldo Sexton Day, Vero Beach, November 5, 1958. COURTESY SEXTON COLLECTION, ARCHIVE CENTER, INDIAN RIVER COUNTY MAIN LIBRARY

OPPOSITE: Welcome Home Veterans after WWII by Florida Sporting Goods, Inc. boat, circa 1947. COURTESY INDIAN RIVER COUNTY HISTORICAL SOCIETY COLLECTION, ARCHIVE CENTER, INDIAN RIVER COUNTY MAIN LIBRARY

ABOVE: Merrill P. Barber receives recognition for his years of service to Indian River County and the state during the Jaycee Park dedication on March 22, 1958. From left: Governor Leroy Collins, Merrill Barber, Louis "Buck" Vocelle, Edgar Schlitt.

COURTESY INDIAN RIVER COUNTY HISTORICAL SOCIETY COLLECTION, ARCHIVE CENTER, INDIAN RIVER COUNTY MAIN LIBRARY

ABOVE LEFT: Indian River Fruit parade float, 1965.

COURTESY INDIAN RIVER PRESS JOURNAL

BELOW LEFT: The Vero Beach High School band marches past the Florida Theatre on 14th Street in the 1950s.

COURTESY INDIAN RIVER COUNTY HISTORICAL SOCIETY COLLECTION, ARCHIVE CENTER, INDIAN RIVER COUNTY MAIN LIBRARY

OPPOSITE: Waldo Sexton Day celebration, Vero Beach, November 5, 1958.

COURTESY SEXTON COLLECTION, ARCHIVE CENTER, INDIAN RIVER COUNTY MAIN LIBRARY

INDEX